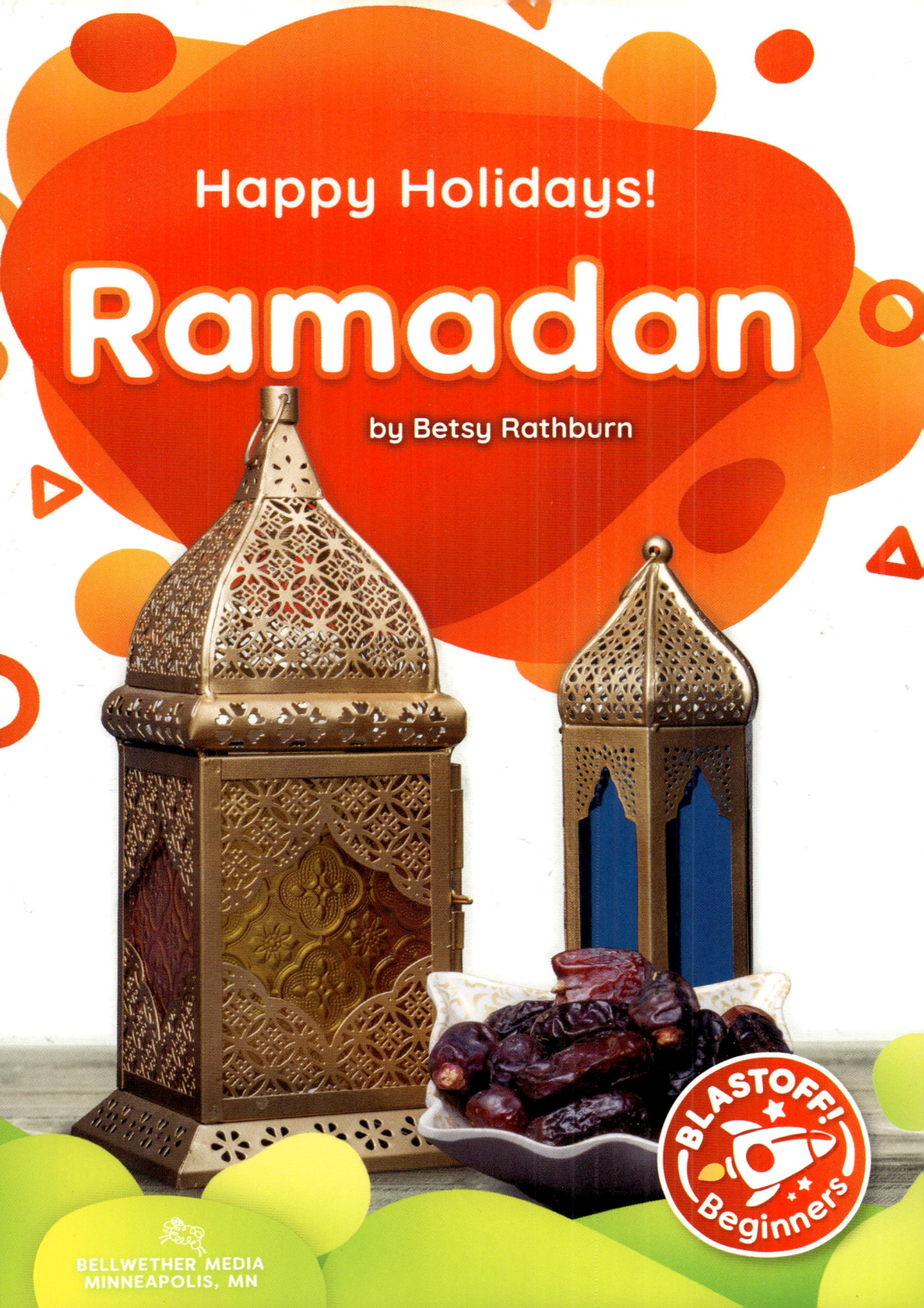

Happy Holidays!
Ramadan
by Betsy Rathburn

BLASTOFF! Beginners

BELLWETHER MEDIA
MINNEAPOLIS, MN

Blastoff! Beginners are developed by literacy experts and educators to meet the needs of early readers. These engaging informational texts support young children as they begin reading about their world. Through simple language and high frequency words paired with crisp, colorful photos, Blastoff! Beginners launch young readers into the universe of independent reading.

Sight Words in This Book

a	big	here	there	we
all	day	is	they	with
and	each	it	time	
at	eat	people	to	
be	first	the	water	

This edition first published in 2023 by Bellwether Media, Inc.

No part of this publication may be reproduced in whole or in part without written permission of the publisher. For information regarding permission, write to Bellwether Media, Inc., Attention: Permissions Department, 6012 Blue Circle Drive, Minnetonka, MN 55343.

Library of Congress Cataloging-in-Publication Data

LC record for Ramadan available at: https://lccn.loc.gov/2022009292

Text copyright © 2023 by Bellwether Media, Inc. BLASTOFF! BEGINNERS and associated logos are trademarks and/or registered trademarks of Bellwether Media, Inc.

Editor: Christina Leaf   Designer: Laura Sowers

Printed in the United States of America, North Mankato, MN.

Table of Contents

It Is Ramadan!	4
A Holy Month	6
A Joyful Time!	12
Ramadan Facts	22
Glossary	23
To Learn More	24
Index	24

It Is Ramadan!

It is dark.
We light a lamp.
Ramadan is here!

lamp

A Holy Month

Ramadan is a **holy** month. The month moves each year.

It is a **Muslim** holiday.

People try to be close to **Allah**. They show kindness.

A Joyful Time!

People **fast** all day. They eat at night.

They eat
a date first.
They drink water.

dates

They meet with friends and family.
They pray.
They eat.

praying

The month ends.
It is Eid al-Fitr!

There is a
big meal.
It is a joyful time!

Ramadan Facts

Celebrating Ramadan

water
lamp
dates

Ramadan Activities

show kindness

eat at night

visit with friends and family

Glossary

Allah

the god of the Islamic faith

fast

to not eat or drink for a certain amount of time

holy

important to a faith

Muslim

related to the Islamic faith

To Learn More

ON THE WEB

FACTSURFER

Factsurfer.com gives you a safe, fun way to find more information.

1. Go to www.factsurfer.com.

2. Enter "Ramadan" into the search box and click 🔍.

3. Select your book cover to see a list of related content.

Index

Allah, 10
dark, 4
date, 14
day, 12
drink, 14
eat, 12, 14, 16
Eid al-Fitr, 18
family, 16
fast, 12

friends, 16
holy, 6
kindness, 10
lamp, 4
light, 4
meal, 20
month, 6, 18
Muslim, 8
night, 12

pray, 16
water, 14

The images in this book are reproduced through the courtesy of: Abu hasim.A, front cover; MidoSemsem, p. 3; Karrrtinki, p. 4; Mrs_ya, pp. 4-5; Mongkolchon Akesin, pp. 6-7; PeopleImages, pp. 8-9; Zuraisham Salleh, pp. 10-11; Edwin Tan, pp. 12-13; Nataly Studio, p. 14; Rawpixel, pp. 14-15; Apiwan Borrikonratchata, p. 16; Odua Images, pp. 16-17, 22 (show kindness, visit with friends and family); GCShutter/ Getty, pp. 18-19; Humba Frame, p. 20; Zurijeta, pp. 20-21; arapix, p. 22; Rawpixel.co, p. 22 (eat at night); Aisylu Ahmadieva, p. 23 (Allah); ZouZou, p. 23 (fast); dieddin, p. 23 (holy); Zurijeta, p. 23 (Muslim).